Forward

The Last Annual Vol State Road Race, what is this event? "The Last Annual" part is a spoof of all the races that were coming out with "The First Annual" back when the race director started the race in 1981.

Vol State is because of the 500km (yes that's about 314 miles) is in the state of Tennessee (The Vol State) although it runs in 5 states total.

The race Starts in Dorena Landing, Missouri and runs about 100 yards down to the ferry that crosses the Mississippi River to Hickman, Kentucky. After leaving Kentucky at about 8 miles the race enters Tennessee near Union City crossing the state exiting it west of Chattanooga entering Alabama for about 3 miles before entering Georgia on a private ranch called Castle Rock for the last 1.3 miles.

The race has also been called "Vacation without a car".

This booklet is an attempt to give most of the pertinent information to the participants in there journey of 100 pies, 100 x PI or 314 miles...

Turn Directions

Turn Sheet
All Miles are from getting OFF the ferry

Start
Follow 1354 Which joins **[.4 mile] SR** 94(Catlett St/Hall St.) along the water. Hall St. becomes Main St. and bears right. The road forks, SR 94 goes right. **[1.2](runners stay LEFT)**runners bear left onto Clinton St. Turning right onto **[1.5]** Kentucky St. then turning left onto Carrol St. at the top of the hill. **The next 3 turns are in very quick succession.** Turn right onto Wabash St. then left onto Mouton St. and another left onto Myatt St which becomes Magnolia St. then a final right onto **[2.1]** Troy St. at the overlook which is SR 125. SR 125 veers left and leaves town.

Hickman thru Union City
Stay on SR 125 till crossing the **[8.5]** state line into Tennessee when the route number changes to SR 5 (same road). Just before Union City SR 5 joins SR 22 and becomes Main St., continue on Main St. at **[14.9]** 5th St Main does a quick right then left continue on Main St. to 3rd St. Turn right on 3rd to the courthouse. Go Clockwise ¼ of the way around the town square turning left exiting the square turning right onto **[15.7]** 1st St. Take a left onto **[16.4]** Reelfoot Ave. (SR 431). On the outskirts of Union City SR 22 joins SR 431. Stay on SR 431 do not get on **[20.0]** SR 22 as it joins from the left and exits on the right, go straight!

Union City thru Martin
Take SR 431 to Martin (SR 431 is Martin Hwy.). On entering Martin SR 431 becomes **[27.7]** University St. Stay on SR 431 thru town as it turns left on **[29.3]** Lindell St. then right on Main St. to Dresden.

Martin thru Dresden

Stay on SR 431 as **[32.6]** SR 22 rejoins continue to Dresden. On coming into Dresden veer left onto **[36.8]** SR 239, Pikeview St. (The sign seems to appear and disappear depending on the year and disposition of the locals) You might find the turns in Dresden marked in big letters by a local, if so, this helps a lot (Dresden is a bit tricky especially if you're going through town after dark and are not fully functional mentally) Turn left onto **[37.5]** W. Main St (SR 89) Turn right on **[38.5]** S. Wilson St., just past the courthouse, and left on **[38.6]** E. Locust St. turn right on to **[38.8]** Linden St. and left on **[39.1]** Evergreen St.. Cross over **[40.5]** SR 22 and leave town. NOTE: If stopping for the night at the motel, you have two choices.

1. Don't turn on Evergreen, staying straight on Linden to SR 22 and left to the motel (this is the shorter route) or make the turn on Evergreen and turn right on SR 22 to the motel (this is about ¼ mile longer but gets you back to the course further along when you leave the motel) either way you MUST backtrack the way you came in back to the course.

Dresden thru McKenzie

Crossing SR 22, Evergreen St. becomes Old Route 22, stay on Old Route 22 all the way into Gleason turning **right on** West St., at the dead end, then left onto **[46.4]** W. Main St. then turn left by the school crossing over the tracks passing the bank with the "time and temperature" display visible. Turn right onto **[46.9]** Cedar St. Passing through the town square. Take Cedar out of town, which becomes Old Route 22 again. Take Old 22 into McKenzie veers right onto **[54.3]** Elm St., then left onto Magnolia St (SR 124) following SR 124 thru town turn right onto **[54.64]** N. Stonewall St (still SR 124) then left onto **[54.88]** Cedar St.. Take Cedar St (still SR 124/22) out of town. You will pass US 79 on the outskirts of town this is mile**[55.6] mile.**

McKenzie Thru Lexington

About 1 1/2 miles past US 79 turn right onto **[57.30]** New SR 22. Take SR 22 all the way to Lexington going right through Huntingdon with no turns (DO NOT take the **[64.0]**bypass around Huntingdon) and past **[80.5]** interstate 40 till you come to **[90.5]** US Route 412 in Lexington. Turn left on US 412 taking it East out of town. (Nice hotel about ¼ mile opposite this, turn west of SR 22 on US 412, it's also been 92 miles which should make a good first day!).

Lexington Thru Columbia

Take US 412 out of Lexington all the way to **[176.0]** Columbia Town Square, about 95 miles, just stay on US 412 (about 1 1/2 mile before the town square it becomes W. 7th St.). Just after passing US 31 in Columbia you turn right at the town square and right again onto Main St. Continue south on Main St. to the dead end then turn right and immediately left onto **[176.4]**US 31 southbound (Carmack Blvd). Continue south on US 31 till it joins **[177.9]** SR 50. Turn left on SR 50 and head out of town.

Columbia To Wartrace

About 5 miles after turning onto SR 50 you will leave SR 50 by turning right onto **[183.0]** SR 373 Culleoka Hwy. Continue on SR 373 till you get to the town square in Lewisburg. **[200.3]** Turn left onto N. 2nd Ave. after about .5 mile there's a split in the road veer right onto Verona Ave.. **[201.3]** US 31A will join you coming in from your right and turning to join you on Verona. Five miles later turn right onto **[206.4]** SR 64 (Shelbyville Hwy.). Take SR 64 all the way to Shelbyville. Coming into Shelbyville you dead end into **[221.8]** US 231. Turn left following both US 231 and SR 64. About .5 mile later turn right onto **[222.4]** W. Holland St. and go to the town square turn right on **[222.6]** Spring St. then immediate left on W. Depot St. taking it through the town square and continuing out of town on SR 64. Crossing **[226.1]**US Rte. 41A continue on SR 64 till you enter Wartrace. After crossing the **[232.1]** railroad tracks turn right onto Church St. then left (no choice here!) onto Main St. SR 269 leaving Wartrace.

Wartrace thru Monteagle

1.6 miles after crossing the tracks in Wartrace you will turn left on **[233.7]** Knob Creek Rd.(leaving SR 269) If you miss this turn feel free to follow the marks on the road to do a loop of the Strolling Jim 40 course for an added 41.2 miles. After crossing the **[238.0]** county line Knob Creek Rd. changes name to Sixteenth Model Rd. same road different name. Continue on Sixteenth Model Rd. till it dead ends into US 41 turn right onto **[243.7]** US 41 (which parallels I-24). After crossing **[248.4]** SR 53 veer left onto **[248.6]** Irwin St. stay on Irwin thru the town square till it rejoins US-41A. Turn left on **[248.8]** US 41 continuing on US 41 all the way to Monteagle (enjoy the last 3 miles, it's a good excuse to walk a bit in case you haven't had to walk yet! It's only the first of two hills in the race). At the top of the hill turn left onto **[273.1]** W. Main St./US 41/SR56.

Monteagle thru Jasper

Continue on Main St. .8 mile and turn left onto **[273.9]** Fairmont Rd (still US 41).1 mile later right onto **[274.0]** Tracy Rd.. Take Tracy Rd/US 41 to Tracy City. In Tracy City turn right onto **[279.6]** Altamont/Main St.(all of this is US 41). Take US 41 out of town. Continue on US 41 to the dead end in **[296.0]** Jasper. Turn right joining US 64. (heading west for the first time!) leaving Jasper.

Jasper to the "ROCK"

Continue on US 64 till crossing under **[300.3]**
I-24, in Kimbal, when it becomes US 72. Follow
US 72 uphill about 1 mile cross to the right side
shoulder and take the exit ramp to **[301.3]** SR 56. Turn
left onto **[302.2]** SR 156 in South Pittsburg. Continue
east on SR 156 turn right onto **[307.4]** SR 377 (10k to
go!and last uphill!). After crossing the **[308.7]**
Alabama state line the route name changes to SR 73.
Turn left onto **[311.1]** CR 132. After entering
[312.3]Castle Rock (and Georgia) turn left onto a dirt
farm road **[312.6]**at the bottom of the hill under the
power line cut. Take this to the top of the hill turn
left on a **[312.9]** dirt road/path (this has a power
transmission tower AT the turn) thru the field. After
crossing the field it enters the **[313.3]** woods. Follow
the trail (take the one that is straight into the
woods, there is one that veers right, Don't veer
right)thru the woods to the finish at the "Rock". Do
not go past the rock and be careful with sprint
finishes. It is about a 100 foot sheer drop about 1
foot past the finish ;-)

Any errors in this is strictly your problem I am not
responsible for any of this (Some just say I'm not
responsible!)

Motels and Services

Motels Churches Cemeteries
Fast Foods   Convenience Stores

Mileage	City	Service	Comments
1.1	Hickman	Cafe	Miss Martha's on right
3.0	Hickman	Gas Station	Little General @ Rte 1099
15.2	Union City	Gas Station	BP
15.4	Union City	Gas Station	Little General
16.4	Union City	Fast Food	Subway + multiple others
18.3	Union City	Gas Station	Little General
22.2	Union City	Store	Outdoor Outfitters AC! East of UC
25.2	Martin	Soda Machine	Left, Charter Cable
27.6	Martin	Store	Wall-Mart
27.7	Martin	Fast Food	Multiple, Both sides
27.7	Martin	Gas Stations	Multiple, Both sides
27.8	Martin	Motel	Econolodge 731-587-4241
27.9	Martin	Motel	Days Inn 731-587-9577
30.3	Martin	Gas Station	JF Quickstop
30.9	Martin	Cafe	Damron's BBQ, on right
32.0	Martin	Cemetery	On Right
38.4	Dresden	Soda	Gas Station with soda machine
38.5	Dresden	Fast Food	Pizza shop on side street, just before Town Square. About 20 meters left of course. Open about 4 to 9 pm
38.7	Dresden	Gas Station	Stay straight instead of turning away from town square. About 50 meters off course.

39.1	Dresden	Motel	Budget Inn 731-364-3152 At turn off for Evergreen St. stay on Linden St. to Rte 22 (about .7 mile) turn left and motel is on your right. Various Fast Foods and convenience stores nearby. You MUST retrace your steps to Evergreen St. to continue. Alternately you could take Evergreen to Rte 22 and backtrack right on Rte 22 about 1 mile to the motel but this is longer.
39.7	Dresden	Church	With neighboring Ball Fields
46.9	Gleason	Grocery	Store on Right with soda machine outside.
46.9	Gleason	Cafe	Across from store. Open 5am-1pm
46.9	Gleason	Gas Station	Turn left at cafe/store and there is a late night gas station visible about ¼ mile down. @ Main & Cedar St.
54.3	McKenzie	Gas Station	Little General @ turn
55.6	McKenzie	Fast Foods	Various both sides of course on US Route 79
55.6	McKenzie	Gas Station	24 hour @ intersection
55.6	McKenzie	Motel	Best Western 731-352-1083 On US Rte 79 About ¼ mile east (left) of course on right.
57.0	McKenzie	Church	On left before Rte 22
59.0	McKenzie	Cemetery	On left side
64.2	Huntingdon	Church	On left side Just past 70A
65.6	Huntingdon	Restaurant	½ block left of course on road when entering town square.
65.8	Huntingdon	Police Office	water and rest rooms 24 hour
65.9	Huntingdon	Cafe	Misty's All Star Cafe on left

66.7	Huntingdon	Motel	Heritage Inn 731-986-2281 Leaving town on the left at inter-section with bypass Rte 70.
67.4	Huntingdon	Church	¾ mile past hotel
69.3	Huntingdon	Soda	On left after entering Rte 22.
70.5	Huntingdon	Church	On left
73.6	Clarksburg	Cemetery	On left just inside city limits
75.0	Clarksburg	Gas Station	On left
75.2	Clarksburg	Store	Dollar General on left
80.5	Parkers Cross-Roads	Fast Foods	Multiple fast foods both sides
80.5	Parkers CR	Motel	Knights Inn 731-968-0759 Before Interstate 40
80.9	Parkers CR	Motel	America's Best Value 731-968-2532 After Interstate 40
85.0	Lexington	Church	On right
85.5	Lexington	Church	On right
86.5	Lexington	Gas Station	Fast Fuels
87.5	Lexington	Gas Station	Fast Fuels
87.7	Lexington	Church	On right
88.6	Lexington	Church	On right
90.5	Lexington	Gas Station	Multiple @ turn onto Rte 431
90.5	Lexington	Fast Food	Various off course at turn
90.5	Lexington	Motel	Off course about 200 meters to right Days Inn 731-968-1997
92.7	Lexington	Gas Station	Little General
98.2	Chesterfield	Convenience	Mom and Pop W/Soda Machine
100.9	Darden	Convenience	Mom and Pop W/Soda Machine
106.0	Parsons	Motel	Parsons Inn 731-847-2378
106.3	Parsons	Gas Station	BP @ main intersection
106.3	Parsons	Fast Food	Subway @ gas station

106.3	Parsons	Motel	Deerfield Inn 731-847-4700 Located off course ¾ mile north of route on Rte 69 various fast foods on the way.
107.5	Parsons	Grocery	Save A Lot
109.3	Parsons	Bar	On right
109.4	Parsons	Bar	On right
110.0	Parsons	Motel	Pine Tree Inn 731-847-4102
110.4	Perryville	Gas Station	Fast Fuel
110.4	Perryville	Restaurant	With gas station
111.0	Perryville	Gas Station	BP
112.6	Perryville	Gas Station	Marathon gas
112.6	Perryville	Restaurant	Fat Man's
116.1	Linden	Cemetery	On left
120.0	Linden	Church	On right (outside water)
123.5	Linden	Gas Station	West side of Linden
124.0	Linden	Motel	Commodore Hotel 931-589-3224
124.2	Linden	Restaurant	Rusty Hook on left at curve in road
124.5	Linden	Gas Station	Leaving town
126.1	Linden	Church	On left
127.5	Linden	Gas Station	Closes at 7:30 to 8:00pm At 'Y' in road make sure you go right here.
134.5	Hohenwald	Gas Station	412 Gas, outskirts of town
137.5	Hohenwald	Church	On left
143.2	Hohenwald	Motel	Embassy Inn 931-796-3587
144.0	Hohenwald	Gas Stations	Various next ½ mile leaving town
144.0	Hohenwald	Fast Foods	Various next ½ mile leaving town
144.5	Hohenwald	Store	Wall-Mart
151.2	Hohenwald	campground	Natchez Trace Campground Office in house behind main building. Very helpful usually has cheap food and soda with free refills
151.9	Hampshire	Church	On right (old church on left)

160.7	Hampshire	Gas Station	Mack's Market opens 7a weekdays 8am on Sat. 1pm on Sunday with soda machine out front
162.9	Hampshire	Cemetery	On right
162.9	Hampshire	Church	On left
172.5	Columbia	Gas Station	Quick Mart E. of Columbia College
173.9	Columbia	Gas Station	Exxon
174.3	Columbia	Fast Food	Hardee's
174.3	Columbia	Gas Station	2 choices
176.0	Columbia	Cafe	On right before town square
177.9	Columbia	Motel	Richland Inn 931-796-3587 off course, straight thru, across Rte 50 on left. About 100 meters off course
178.5	Columbia	Gas Station	
178.9	Columbia	Gas Station	
183.2	Glendale	Gas Station	"Bench Of Despair" 5am-6pm
187.5	Culleoka	Gas Station	With nice sit down cafe
192.9	Mooreville	Gas Station	On right
198.5	Lewisburg	Grocery	Grocery/Pharmacy on left
199.0	Lewisburg	Gas Station	On right
201.4	Lewisburg	Restaurant	Huddle House on right after light
201.4	Lewisburg	Gas Station	Various
201.8	Lewisburg	Motel	Celebration Inn 931-359-7490 About ¼ mile past light leaving town. On Course.
206.0	Farmington	Convenience	White's Market (no rest rooms)
207.3	Farmington	Church	Defunct, on left
211.6	Wheel	Church	On right, in Wheel
213.7	Wheel	Gas Station	About 2 miles past Wheel on left
215.3	Bedford	Gas Station	Bedford Market Soda Machine
221.8	Shelbyville	Gas Station	Convenience Store at turn 24 hour
222.0	Shelbyville	Motel	Magnolia Inn

222.4	Shelbyville	Motel	America's Best Value 931-684-6050 About 1/3 mile past turn to go up to the town square. Various Fast Food and Gas Stations along motel route
222.8	Shelbyville	Cafe	50's and Fiddles (great shakes)
226.0	Shelbyville	Gas Station	Corner of US41 & Rte 64
232.0	Wartrace	Gas Station	Marathon Gas
240.2	Wartrace	Church	On left
242.9	Manchester	Campground	Whispering Oaks, Soda Machines
245.0	Manchester	Gas Station	By state park
248.0	Manchester	Convenience	
248.9	Manchester	Motel	Park Inn 931-728-2058
249.0	Manchester	All services	249 – 252 multitude of everything
251.4	Manchester	Motels	Before Interstate 24 crossing Days Inn 931-728-9530 Country Inn 931-728-7551 Americas Best Value 931-728-5177 After Interstate 24 crossing Quality Inn 931-728-0800 Scottish Inn 931-728-0506 Motel 6 931-728-5257 Holiday Inn 931-728-9383
252.0	Manchester	Store	Wall-Mart
256.6	Hillsboro	Soda	Soda Machine
256.9	Hillsboro	Soda	Soda Machine
257.1	Hillsboro	Convenience	On right
266.1	Pelham	Cafe	On left
266.4	Pelham	Cafe	On Left
266.4	Pelham	Convenience	On right Mom & Pop
266.8	Pelham	Cemetery	On left
267.9	Pelham	Church	On left

273.1	Monteagle	All Services	Various Fast Food Convenience Both sides of interstate between ¼ and ½ mile to right off course
273.1	Monteagle	Motels	East side American Eagle 931-924-8880 West Side Super 8 931-924-2222 Mountain Inn 931-924-2221
273.2	Monteagle	Pharmacy	On right after turn
275.0	Monteagle	Gas Station	On left
278.6	Tracy City	Soda	Soda Machine on right
279.4	Tracy City	Gas Station	On right
279.4	Tracy City	Store	Dollar General on left
296.2	Jasper	Gas Station	Exxon on left
299.9	Kimball	Motel	Super 8 423-837-7185
300.0	Kimball	Motel	Comfort Inn 423-837-2479
300.1	Kimball	Motel	America's Best Value 423-837-7933
300.1	Kimball	Fast Food	Wendy's McDonald's Various
300.1	Kimball	Convenience	Various
303.6	New Hope	Convenience	On right
305.7	New Hope	Convenience	On right

Equipment

What I Need

One of the most common questions from first time "The Last Annual Vol State Road Race" participants is "What do I need to carry?".
The following is MY opinion as to what is essential and what is nice to have and what is ridiculous to carry.
None of it is mandatory, but it is mandatory to check in with race management twice a day at approximately 7:30 am and pm...

Essentials
1. Water
2. Cash
3. Drivers License
4. Credit Card
5. ATM Card
6. Cell Phone

Nice To Have
1. Change of Socks
2. Rain Protection
3. Basic Medical Items
4. Body Glide (or equivalent)
5. Small umbrella (works great for sun protection)
6. Battery powered cellphone charger
7. Maps/Documentation
8. Personal hygiene
9. Light weight ground cloth

Ridiculous
1. Multiple changes of clothes
2. Entertainment devices
3. Books
4. Most food
5. Anything over a couple ounces of weight
6. Spare shoes

Remember you have to carry everything for 314 miles and it gets heavy after a few miles!

Rules

Basic Rules

"The Last Annual Vol State Road Race" has three divisions.
1. Relay
2. Solo Competitor with crew
3. Solo Competitor without crew (self-supported)

Below is a list of the basic rules covering the race.
The race intentionally keeps rules to a minimum relying on common sense.
These rules are not all inclusive and the RD is the final authority on any situation.
Runners must cover entire course on their own two feet (hands or knees).

Relay:
All relay members must ride the ferry at the start (or official start if the ferry isn't running).
Relay teams may leave the course at any time but must return and continue from the point they left off.

Solo Crewed:
Runner may leave course at anytime as long as they continue where they left off.
Runner may get in their crew vehicle any time either to get a break from the heat or travel to food/lodging etc as long as they continue from where they leave off.
No receiving of aid from a moving vehicle.
NO Pacers

Solo Self-supported:
Solo runners may not accept aid from anyone associated with the race except for other self-supported runners. This includes personal friends, race management and others such as Ultralisters that have heard about the race and came out to spectate.
Solo self-supported runners may accept aid from locals and other passerby's who randomly meet you on the road.
Self-supported may not get in or on a vehicle at any time during they race except when requested by law enforcement.
Note this does not mean law enforcement offering a ride but basically required by law enforcement.
Runners may NOT cache supplies before hand.

Runners may drop off supplies with race management or crews but cannot get them back till after the finish.

Self-supported runners if they run into trouble may accept aid if needed but will there after be considered Crewed, But they may finish the race.

If two runners (either Solo or Crewed) can not finish by themselves they may join together to form a relay, mid race, as long as all 'members' of the relay started the race at the ferry. NO Pacers!

The following is the race directors definition of pacer/pacing.

Definition of PACER: any accompanying person in the immediate presence of the participant;
running, walking, or riding any mechanical or motorized transport,with the exception of bona fide competitors,
who have also covered the entire distance from the ferry to the point of accompaniment on foot.

Participants who have dropped, finished, or are otherwise not at the same point in the race as the accompanied runner, will be considered as PACERS.

Crew members may accompany their runner, in the performance of their crewing duties, for no more than 100 yards at any given time. this is not to be construed as meaning 100 yards out of every mile.

the intent of the rule against PACERS should be readily apparent, and any contrivance to adhere to the letter of the rule,
while violating its intent, will be considered a violation.
likewise, any incidental violation of the letter of the rule,
clearly without violating the intent, will be considered as adherence.

These are the basics. Use common sense the intent is to cover the course using only foot transport, to cover the whole intended course, and to do it on your own.

Contacts

Contact	Phone Number

Contact	Phone Number

Contact	Phone Number

Contact	Phone Number

Maps

 Motel

 Cafe/Restaurant

 Convenience Store
Gas Station

 Soda Machine

 Pizza

 Cemetery

 Church

 Airport

 North Direction

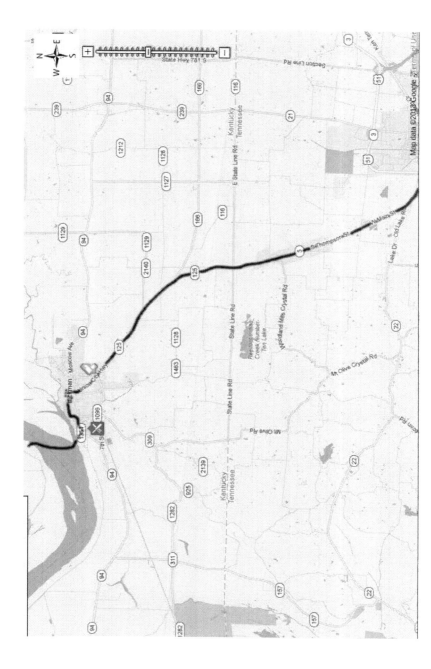

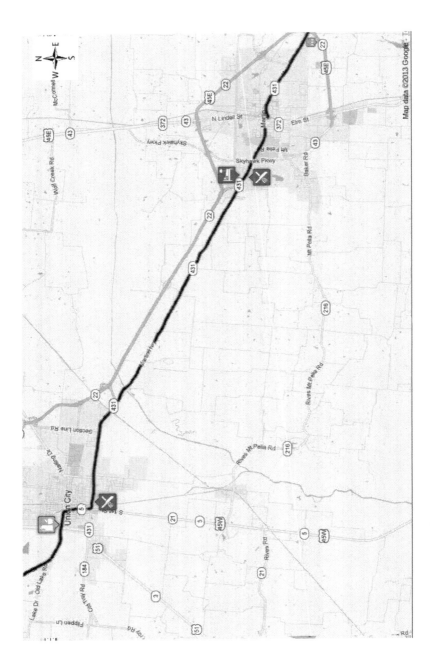

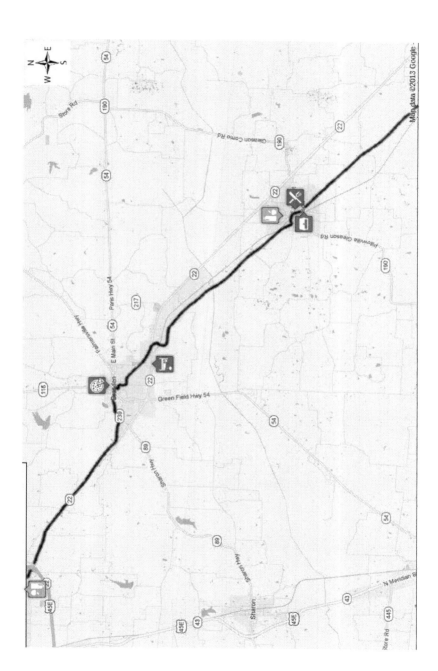

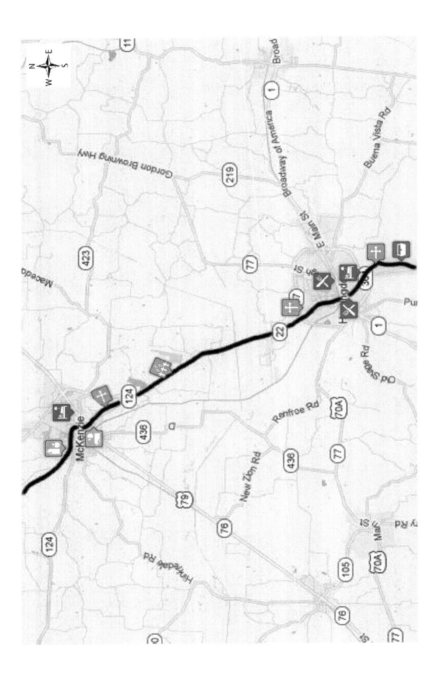

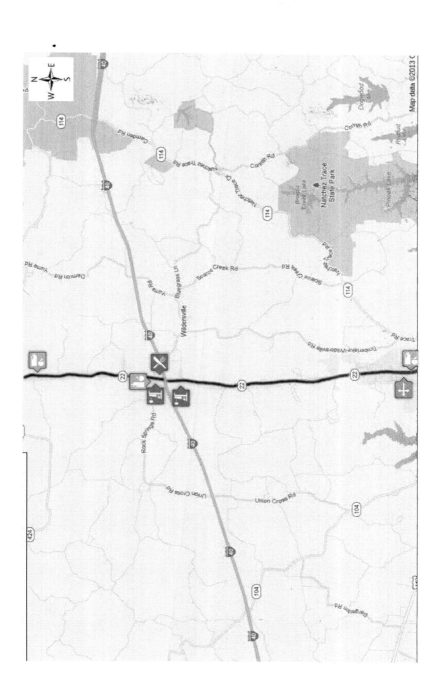

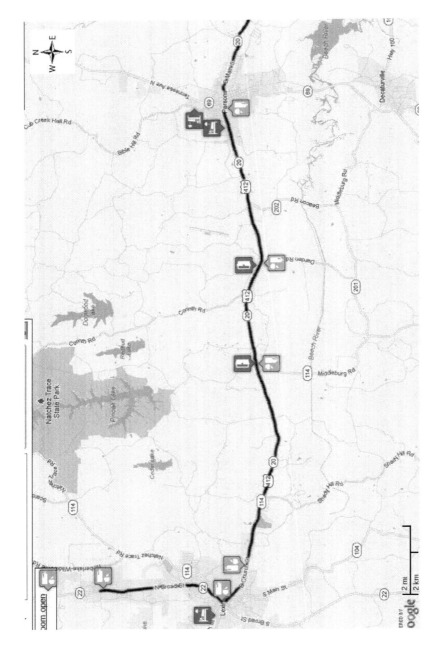

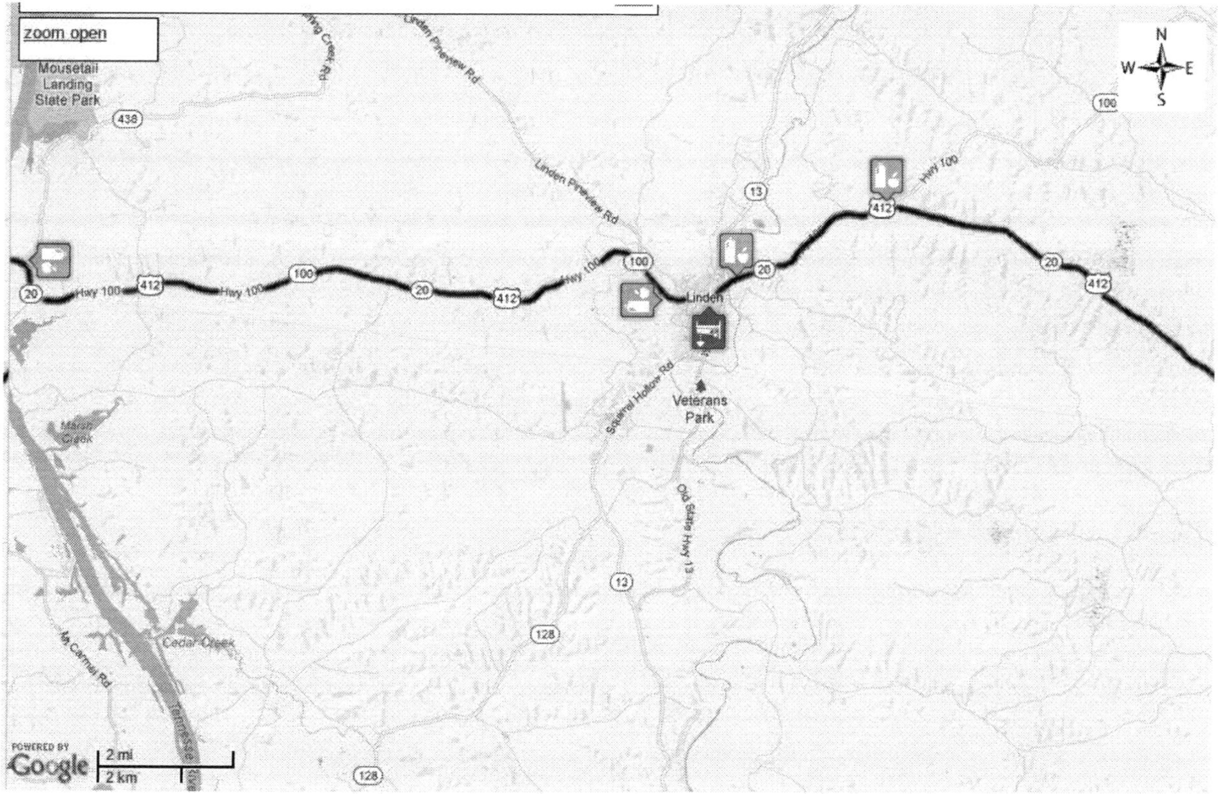
zoom open
Mousetail Landing State Park
Linden Pineview Rd
Hwy 100
Linden
Veterans Park
Squirrel Hollow Rd
Old State Hwy 13
Marsh Creek
Cedar Creek
Mt Carmel Rd
N
W
E
S
POWERED BY Google
2 mi
2 km

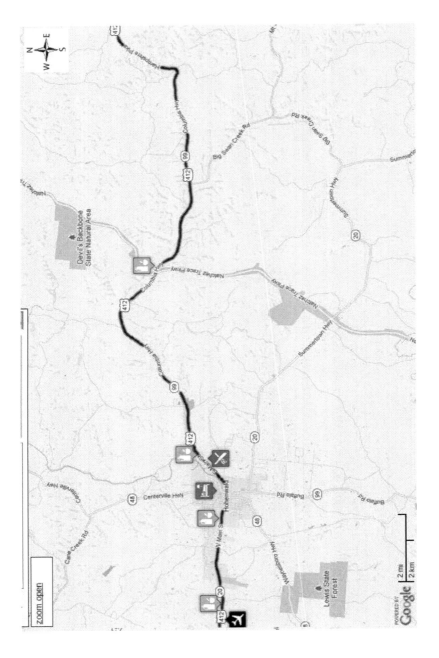

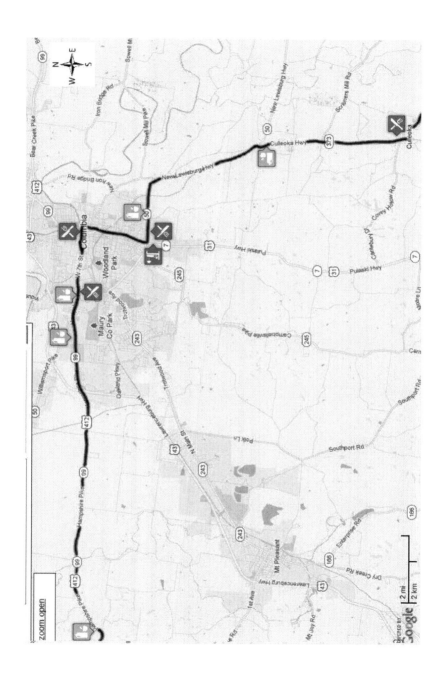

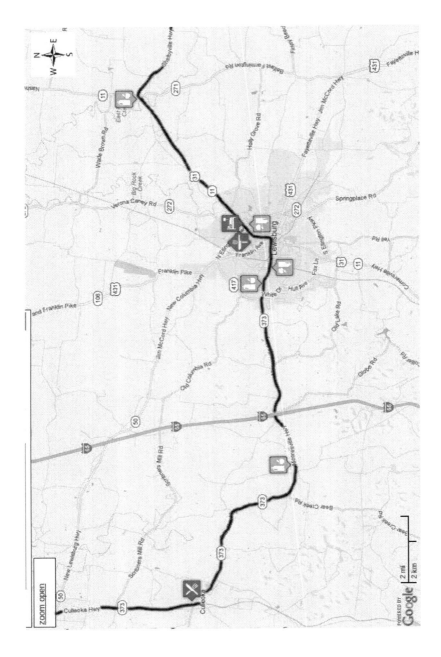

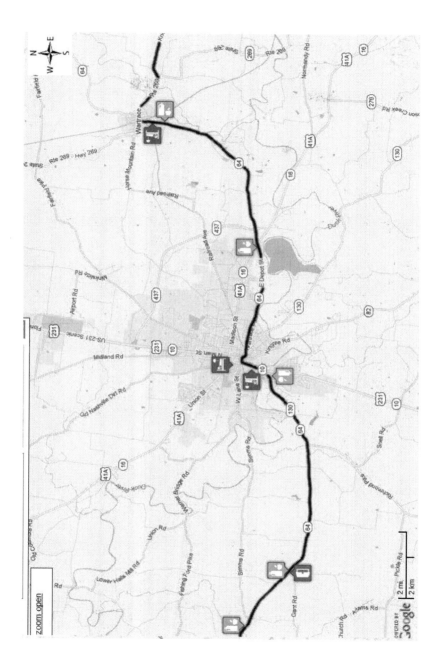

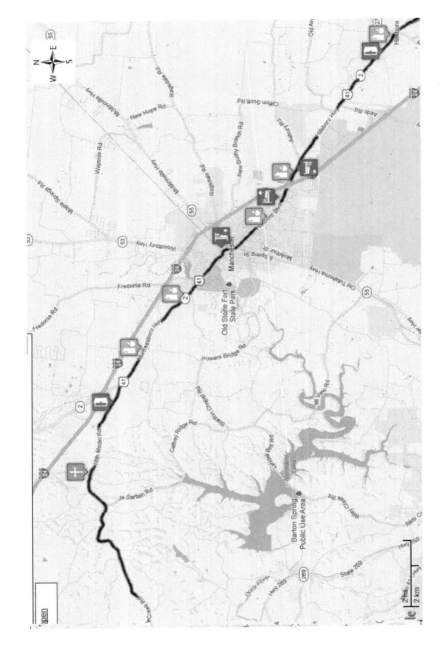

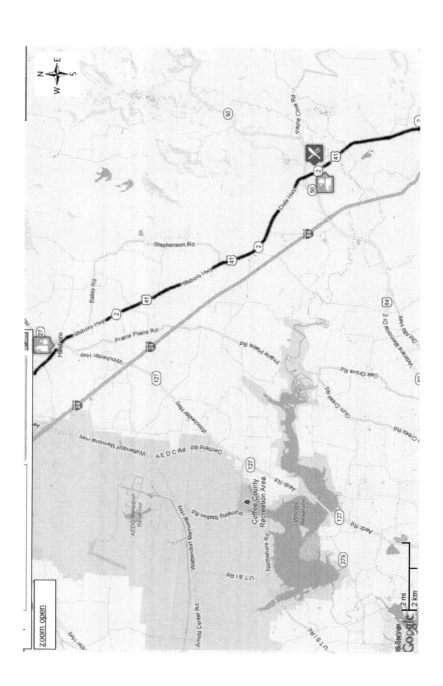

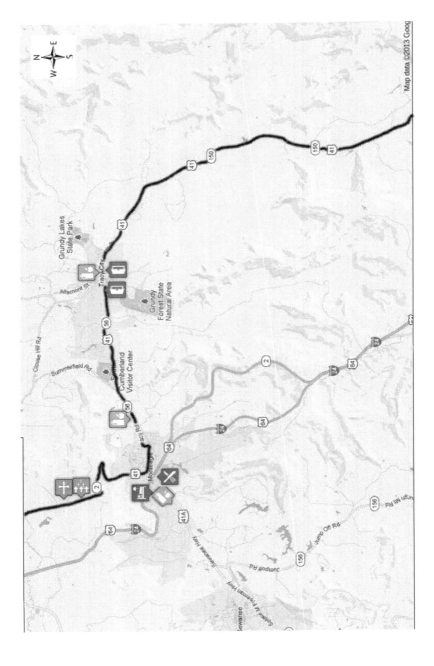

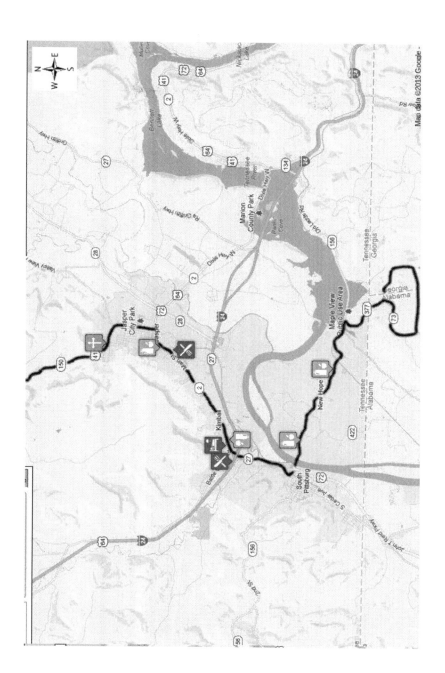

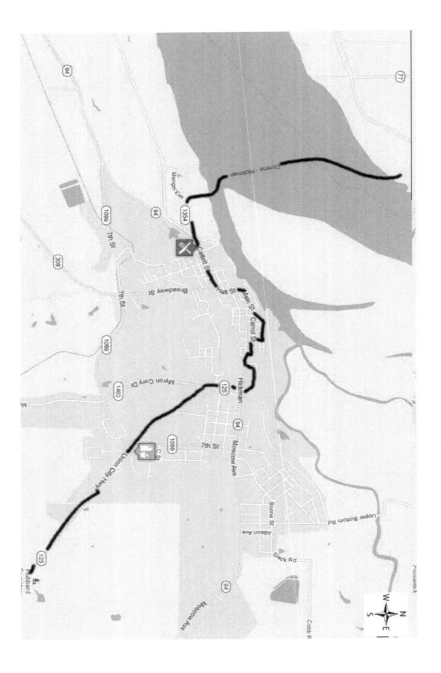

Map data ©2013 G

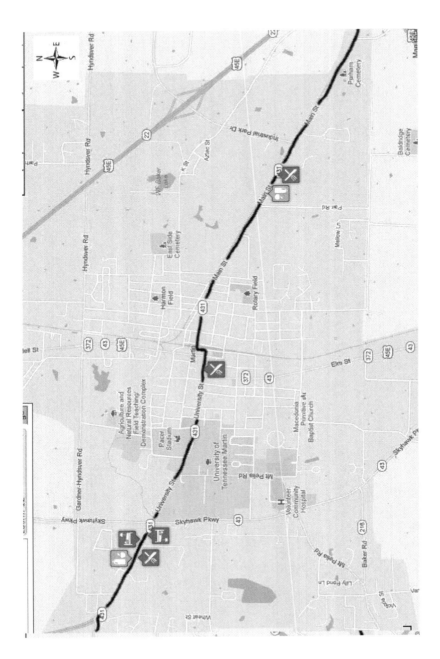

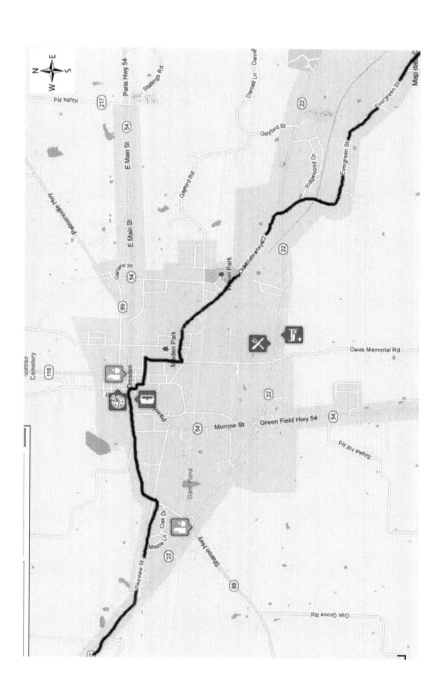

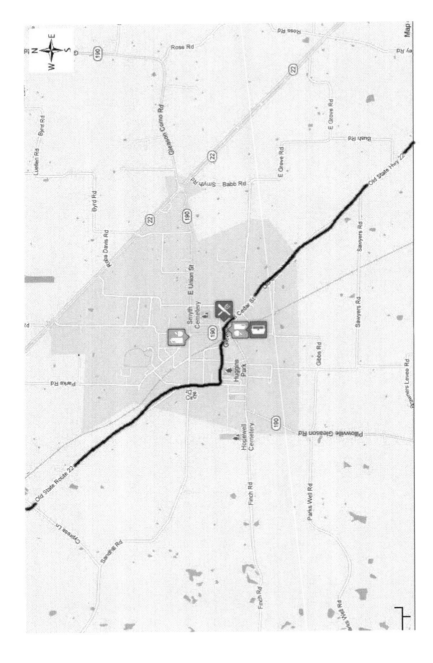

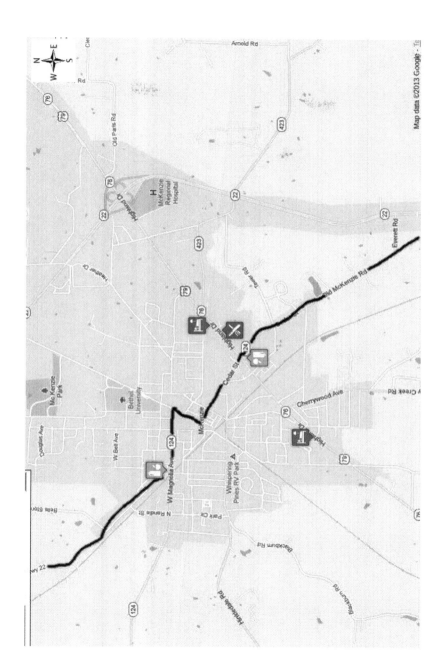

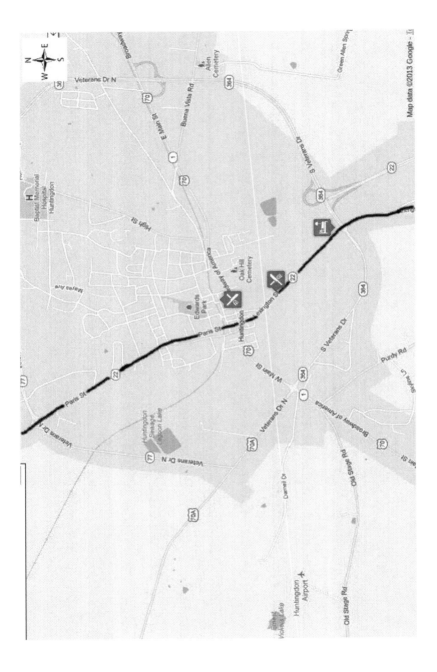

N
W E
S

Aberdeen Rd
Oak Grove Rd
Oak Grove Rd
Davi
412
Harmon Rd
Pope Rd
Timber Valley Cir
39
Reynolds Rd
Pope Rd
Moose Lodge Rd
Saddle Brook Rd
112
Roy Pruitt Rd
Dickson Ln
Leola Dr
26
Hedgewood Dr
Church St
City Park
Natchez Trace Dr
114
Hall St
Hamlet St
112
Cleaner St
22
N Broad St
114
114
114
22
114
20
104
S Main St
47
Lexin
20
S Broad St
W Church St
22
Barnett St
Decatur St
112
ch River
aterfowl
elopment
Rd

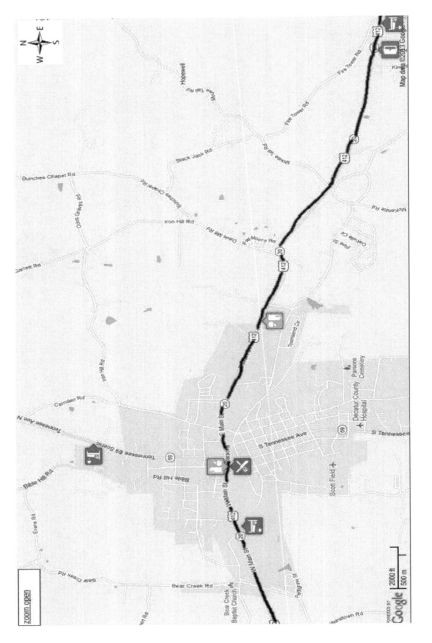

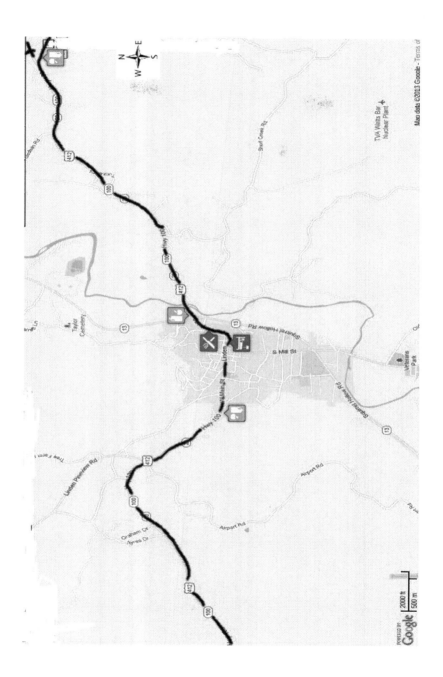

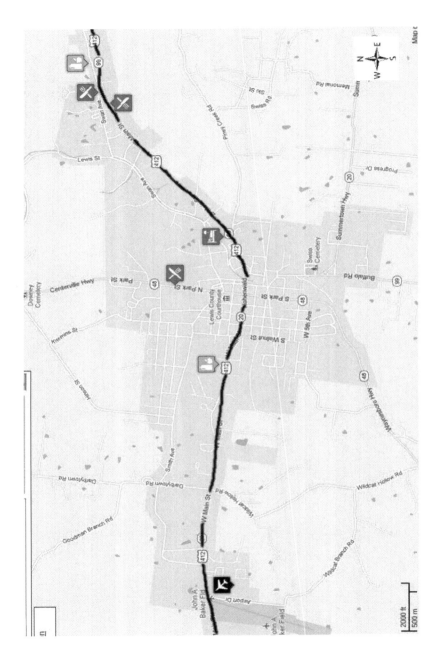

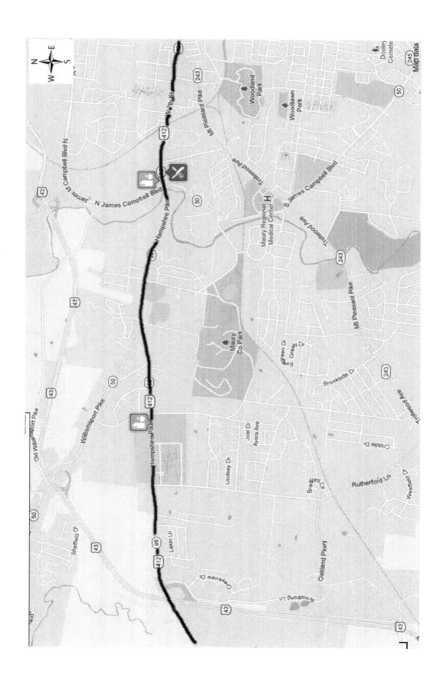

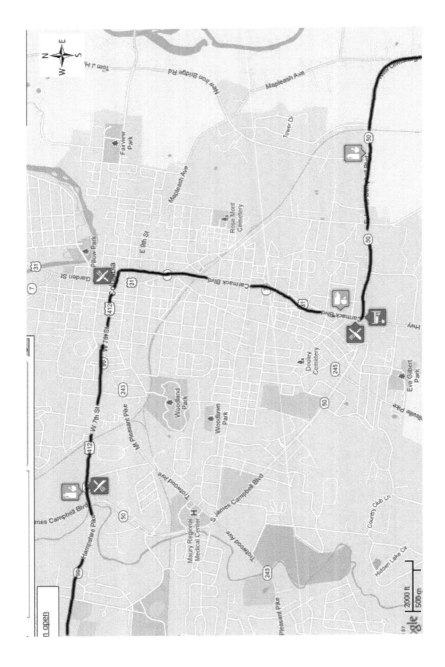

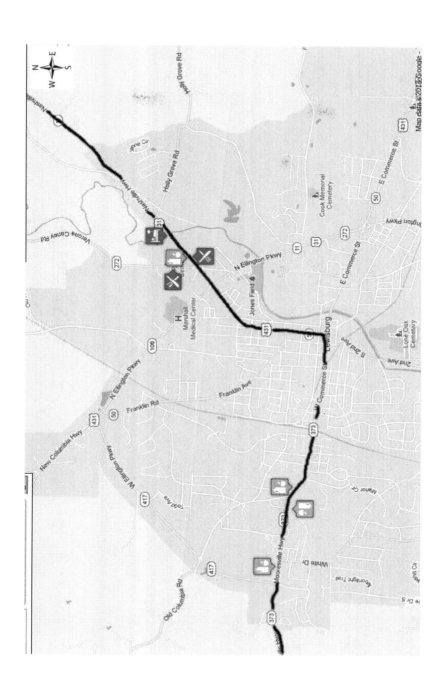

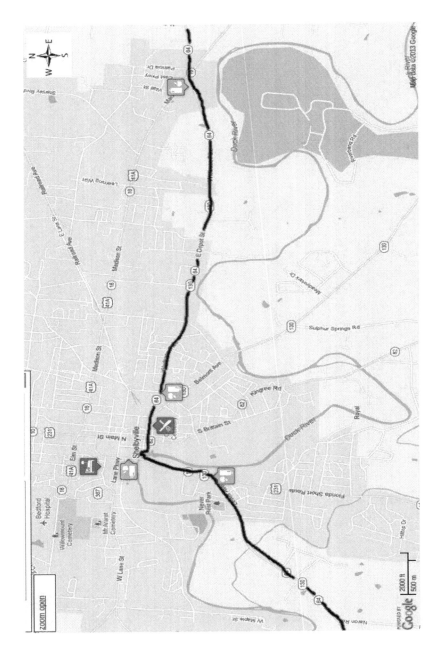

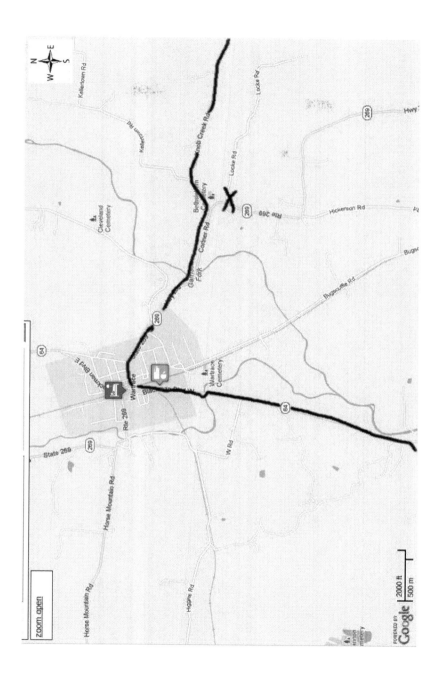

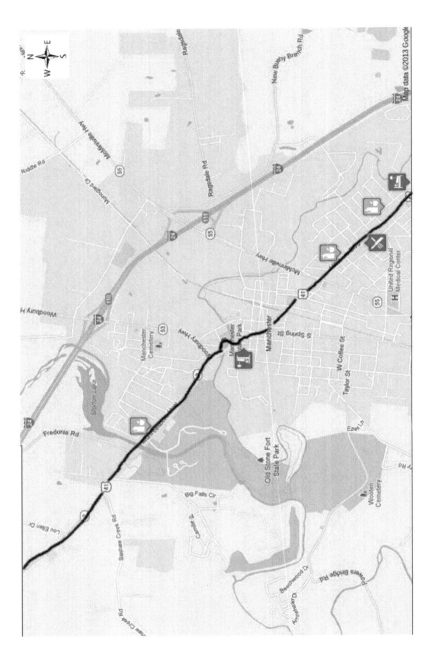

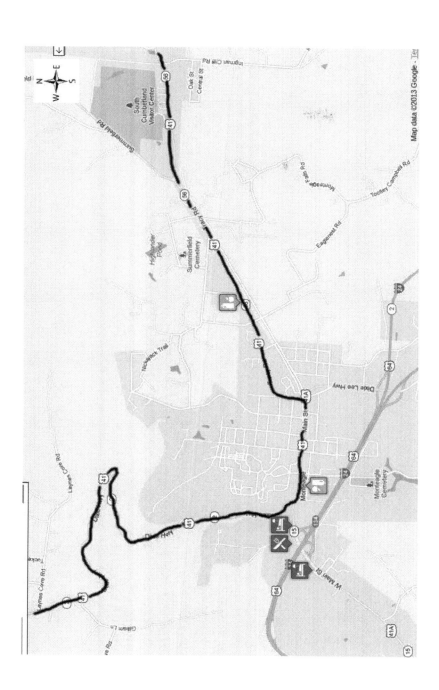

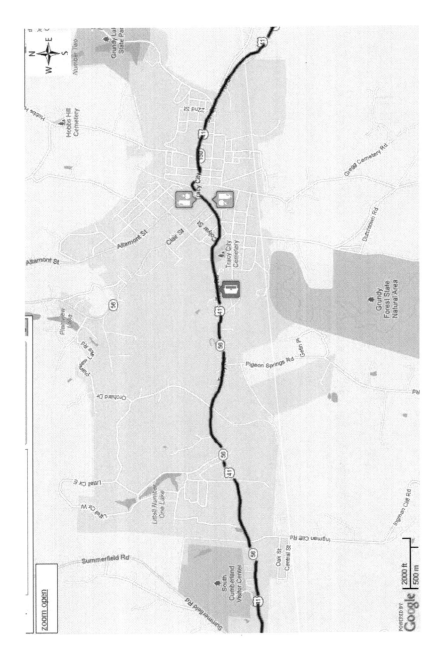

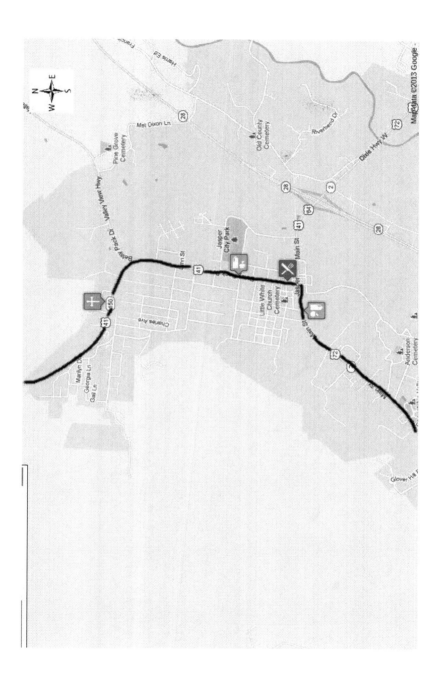

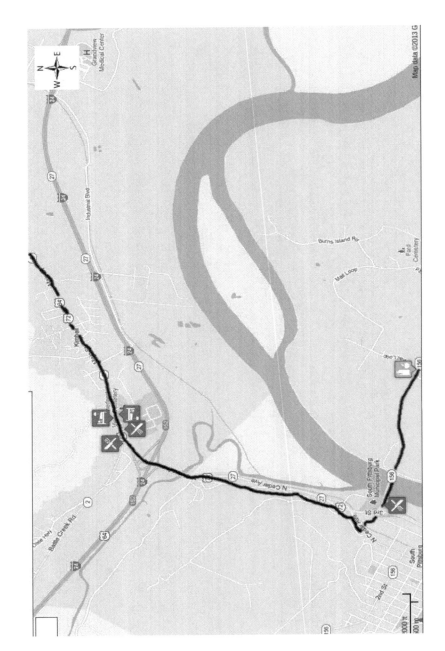

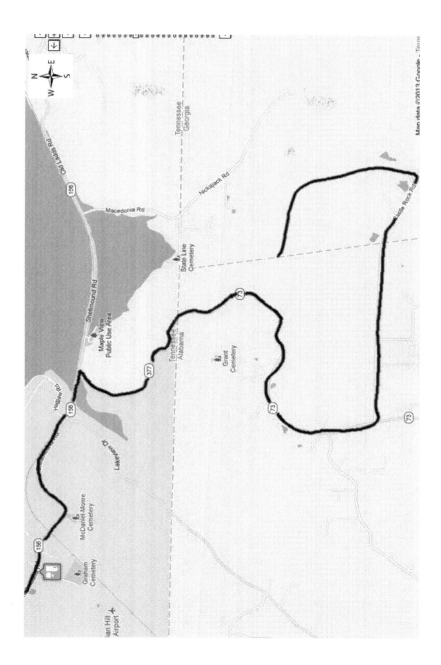